RAISING TOMORROW'S LEADERS

Raising Tomorrow's Leaders

CA Garjana Rathore

Contents

Dedication viii

Acknowledgement ix

Book Reviews xi

Foreword xiii

Foreword xvii

1 Introduction 1

2 Parenting Lessons from the 1983 Cricket World Cup 6

3 A Letter from the Heart 13

4 Parenting the Krishna Way 18

5 Krishna – A Guide Amidst the Storm 25

6 The Race We Never Chose 30

7 The Leap Year Gift – One Extra Day to Love 35

8 A Mother's Nurturing Touch 40

9 The Power of One More Push 44

10 That Little Extra Push is a Key to Your Success 49

11 Give Wings to Fly and Let Her Soar 54

12 Push Beyond the Limits – A Ride into the Unknown 58

13 Unlearn Parenting – The Mission Mangal Way 64

14 Conclusion 72

15 Book References 75

16 Recommended Reading List 77

17 Find Me Here 80

First Printing, 2025

Dedication

This book is dedicated to the mothers who've tucked away dreams to make room for someone else's, and to the fathers who hold back their tears to stay strong for the kids.

To my children whose journey into the world taught me how to see it through new eyes. And to the children who will one day lead this world with heart, hope, and honour- this book is for you.

Acknowledgement

I was blessed to grow up in the embrace of a joint family, where love and discipline moved in perfect harmony. My grandmother's scoldings with unspoken care and my father's boundless pampering taught me the delicate art of "Balance"—a lesson that became the heartbeat of this book!

With my grandparents, parents, uncles, and aunts, my place was a symphony of security that cocooned me as a child, and I learned what it means to be nurtured - a gift I have strived to pass on to my children and to this book.

Fortune smiled upon me again when I married in a joint family, welcoming me with the same warmth and love I had known in my childhood. It is the foundation upon which this book stands, and for that, I am eternally grateful.

To Vikas, my best half, for sharing this wild, beautiful journey of parenthood.

To my children, Sakshi and Saksham—thank you for choosing me to be your mother. Respecting my work commitments and lending a hand in responsibilities, you have redefined the same art of "Balance". More than two decades of parenting now feels like a quick flash. There is so much more I want to teach you, so much more I long to share.

Even as you grow, a piece of my parenting heart will always beat for you, guiding and growing for the rest of my days.

This book is for every parent who pours their heart into raising their children. It is for those who, like me, find joy in the small moments, strength in the challenges, and purpose in the endless journey of parenthood. May these words resonate with you, like they do with me, as a celebration of the love we give and the lessons we learn along the way.

With love
Garjana

Book Reviews

"A Parenting Game-Changer!"

This book beautifully blends wisdom from sports, spirituality, and real-life struggles. Each chapter offers profound yet practical lessons. Perfect for parents, educator, mentor who want to raise resilient, emotionally intelligent kids.

By Manoj Sonawane, Author of the Book "Learning 2.0"

"A Book I'll Re-Read for Years"

Blends storytelling, psychology, and heart. The "Push Beyond Limits" chapter motivated me to challenge my own fears. Brilliant!

Happy Reading!

By Hemsingh Patle, author of the book "The Five Minutes Magical Habits."

Foreword

To embrace parenthood is to step onto a remarkable, often unpredictable terrain. It's a landscape painted with vibrant highs, unexpected detours, and a quiet, profound realization that the learning never truly ends. We often begin with a mental sketch of perfection, only to discover that authentic connection, not flawless execution, is the true masterpiece we're meant to create.

This profound truth is precisely why I am so genuinely thrilled for you to experience CA Garjana Rathore's insightful new book, *Raising Tomorrow's Leaders.* I've consistently been captivated by her unique blend of sharp intellect and deep emotional intelligence. As a Chartered Accountant by profession, she possesses an extraordinary capacity to dissect complex realities and present them with crystalline clarity. Yet, in her approach to raising her own children, I've seen her seamlessly weave this precision with a heartfelt understanding of human nuance, a truly rare alchemy.

In the book, Garjana distils her rich experience, diligent research, and unfiltered observations into a companion you'll find indispensable. This isn't a rigid blueprint demanding adherence to a single doctrine; rather, it's a thoughtfully designed compass, offering a multitude of paths and perspectives for your individual journey. You'll particularly appreciate her profound message that a child's inherent worth and potential are never tied to specific achievements. Instead, she champions the vital role of unwavering encouragement, emphasizing how nurturing a child's spirit, even when they don't excel, builds the deepest foundations for their future growth and confidence. Within these pages, you'll uncover innovative mental frameworks for fostering resilience, practical strategies to navigate daily emotional currents with greater ease, and powerful prompts to deepen genuine communication within your family.

What truly elevates this work is her authentic voice, a comforting presence that understands the quiet anxieties, celebrates the exhilarating breakthroughs, and honors the simple, profound beauty that defines the parenting experience. Reading this book feels less like receiving instructions and more like engaging in a candid, insightful conversation with a wise friend who genuinely champions your growth.

Whether you're just charting your course into parenthood, seeking renewed energy amidst its demands, or simply yearning to cultivate a richer, more harmonious bond with the young lives in your care, *Raising Tomorrow's Leaders* will become a treasured guide. It moves beyond conventional advice; it's a heartfelt invitation to embrace the reality of parenting with deeper intention, greater presence, and an overflowing measure of joy.

Prepare to feel enlightened, affirmed, and wonderfully poised to navigate the magnificent odyssey of raising confident, compassionate individuals.

Warmly,
By Dr. Sonal Sisodia
Academician

Foreword

Some books inform! Some inspire! But then, there are a rare few that wrap around your heart like a warm embrace and whisper, "You're not alone." This is one of those rare ones.

When my dear friend set out to write this book, she didn't just pen down parenting tips — she poured her soul into every word. These pages carry the wisdom and experience of a mother, the honesty of a seeker, and the simplicity of someone who has truly lived every moment she writes about.

Parenting, we often believe, is about children. But this book gently reminds us — it's also about us. It is about growing, unlearning, accepting imperfections, laughing through chaos, and finding beauty in bedtime battles and banana-peel mornings.

Through her words, my friend becomes a companion to every parent — not a preacher from a pedestal, but a partner on the path. Her stories are real, her voice is reassuring, and her reflections are refreshingly relatable.

To my dearest friend Garjana — thank you. For writing from your truth. For letting your heart be seen. And for gifting the world something that will comfort, connect, and celebrate parenthood in all its messy, magical glory.

This book is not a manual. It's a mirror. And every parent who looks into it will feel a little more understood.

With love, pride, and deep admiration,
CA Ishani Maheshwari

1

Introduction

The way we talk to our children becomes their inner voice."- Peggy O'Mara

Parenting is one of life's most profound responsibilities. In a world that is rapidly evolving, driven by technological advances, global challenges, and shifting values, raising children who are resilient, emotionally intelligent, and grounded in strong ethics has never been more vital.

"Raising Tomorrow's Leader" is not just a parenting guide; it's a journey through real-life reflections, stories, and values that inspire purposeful parenting. Each chapter in this book offers insights drawn, cultural narratives and personal experiences, crafted to help you instill confidence, compassion, and courage in your children.

Take, for example, the 1983 Indian Cricket World Cup victory—a story of self-belief, strategy, and perseverance. The Indian team, considered underdogs, rose to create history not through resources, but through belief and resilience. This story isn't just a sports triumph—it's a parenting blueprint. It reminds us to encourage our children to believe in their dreams, even when the odds are stacked against them. Let them fall, let them rise but let them believe.

In another chapter, the act of riding 300 kilometers on a bicycle in one night becomes a metaphor for emotional endurance. It teaches us that parenting requires persistence, even when we are mentally and physically exhausted. We are not perfect, but every step forward in the face of fatigue models resilience for our children.

EVERYDAY WISDOM FROM UNEXPECTED PLACES

Inspiration for parenting doesn't always come from parenting books. Sometimes it comes from unexpected places, like the movie *Mission Mangal.* Through the lens of India's space scientists, we explore themes of trust, letting children make their own choices, and guiding without controlling. Just as the protagonist's mother, Tara, supports her teenage son through his spiritual exploration without judgment, we are reminded that being a parent means being a calm guide, not a dictator.

In the chapter *"Wings to Fly"*, we look at the journey of a mother who once compromised her own dreams but now chooses to give her daughter the freedom and tools to chase hers. It's a reminder that as parents, we must not clip the wings of our daughters or sons with fear or outdated norms. Instead, we must be the wind beneath them.

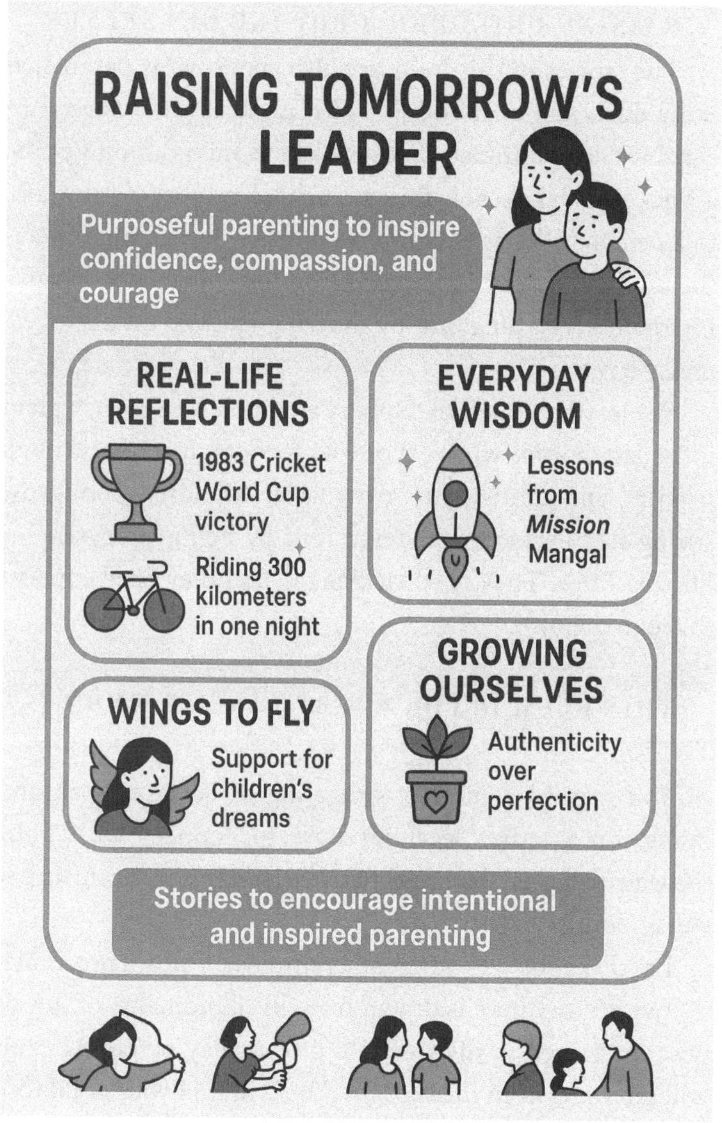

Figure 1: Raising Tomorrow's Leader

RAISING CHILDREN, GROWING OURSELVES

The stories in this book are also about us, as parents, as individuals still evolving. In *"Live as Parents, Not Super Parents,"* we are reminded that it's okay to miss out on getting a cricket match ticket, forget a school project, or say "no" to a demand. What children need is not perfection, but authenticity. They need to know we love them not by giving them everything, but by showing up even on our tired, messy days.

We learn through metaphors as simple as a money plant in a glass bottle, where those with roots, formed through pruning and gentle pain, grow faster. Children, too, grow strong not by being sheltered, but by being prepared for life's realities. They need challenges, and they need support through them.

THIS BOOK IS FOR EVERY PARENT WHO TRIES

You may be a mother struggling to balance work and home, or a father learning how to connect with your teenage daughter. You may feel lost, frustrated, or unsure if you're doing it right.

Let this book be your gentle reminder: you are not alone.

Every story here is drawn from lived moments of joy, of wisdom gained in the trenches of everyday parenting. You will see yourself in these pages. You will find your child too.

So let's begin this journey not toward perfect parenting, but toward intentional, inspired, and emotionally rooted parenting. Let's raise a generation that doesn't just aim to succeed, but to lead with heart, with courage, and with grace.

Let us begin this journey of empowering our children, one value at a time.

2

Parenting Lessons from the 1983 Cricket World Cup

"The first and greatest victory is to conquer yourself." - Plato

Cricket holds a deep, sentimental value in India, uniting generations and communities like no other sport. The 1983 Cricket World Cup victory serves as an inspiring example, offering valuable lessons in resilience, leadership, and belief for both cricket fans and parents. The Indian team's journey from underperformer to champion provides profound insights into parenting. Let's learn about it in this chapter.

Believe in the Dream

We often hear the adage: *"It is not the strongest or bravest team that wins, but the one that believes in its dream."* The 1983 Indian team exemplified this, as they were one of the lowest-ranked teams in the world, participating only due to a change in format. They were ranked below Zimbabwe and had previously struggled in two World Cups, only defeating an East African team. This victory underscores the importance of teaching children to maintain high spirits and believe in their dreams.

For parents, this is a powerful lesson. Teach your children to dream boldly, even when the odds are stacked against them. Encourage them to embrace challenges with unwavering belief in their potential. Success begins not with resources or rankings, but with an unshakable faith in one's ability to overcome obstacles.

Rising Above Adversity

Competing in England, a nation that had ruled India for 200 years, the Indian team's rise in cricket mirrored the country's growing self-belief as it emerged from the shadows of colonial rule and the traumas of partition.

The team lacked resources, including a strong coach and clear strategies. However, Captain Kapil Dev emerged as a key planner and strategist, understanding his players well. In the finals, he advised a bowler to avoid targeting a weak fielder, highlighting the necessity of strategy and teamwork for success.

Parents, like captains, must guide their children through life's complexities, emphasizing preparation, strategy, and collaboration. Sometimes, it's not about having all the answers but knowing how to use available resources wisely.

Perseverance Over Perfection

The team's start was disastrous, suffering a loss in a practice match and performing poorly, until the Indian team defeated the West Indies in their opening match in Manchester. This victory taught that it's not the start that matters, but the ability to maintain faith, hope, and persistence despite setbacks.

Children must learn that life is not a smooth road. Teach them to embrace failures as stepping stones to greatness. Instill in them the value of persistence, showing that every challenge conquered builds strength for the next.

The Power of Self-Belief

The self-belief was crucial in this World Cup, with Kapil motivating his team to aim for victory—an idea initially met with skepticism. A pivotal moment occurred against Zimbabwe when India lost five wickets for just 17 runs, but Kapil's remarkable 175 runs led them to victory. His aggressive leadership and insistence on perseverance transformed the team's confidence. Once they believed in themselves, they began to win consistently. It's essential for a leader to understand and inspire their team.

As parents, fostering self-belief in your children is one of the greatest gifts you can offer. Encourage them to see beyond failures, to believe in their unique abilities, and to lead with conviction. Confidence is a foundation for growth, enabling them to tackle challenges head-on.

Decisions of the Heart

The 1983 victory reminds us that while logic and planning are crucial, the heart often holds the key to extraordinary decisions. Kapil's boldness, at times driven by instinct rather than reason, brought out the best in his team. This line perfectly matches this spirit: *"People may mock you, but while the brain offers options, the heart makes the decision."*

Parents should inspire their children to trust their instincts and embrace emotional intelligence. Life's most meaningful choices often require listening to the heart, for it is the compass that guides us toward our true purpose.

A Legacy of Transformation

The 1983 World Cup victory did more than bring home a trophy—it transformed Indian cricket forever. The team's success sparked a cultural shift, elevating the sport and uniting the nation in pride. More importantly, it taught a generation that success demands a blend of desire, dedication, and strategic planning.

As parents, let this legacy inspire you to instill similar values in your children. Teach them to dream big, persevere through challenges, trust their instincts, and embrace teamwork. Success is not an accident; it is the culmination of belief, effort, and vision.

The 1983 Cricket World Cup is more than a historic achievement—it is a masterclass in resilience, leadership, and self-discovery. Let its lessons resonate in your parenting journey, guiding your children to greatness, one dream at a time.

Figure 2: Parenting Lessons From the 1983 World Cup

Key Points on Leadership:

True leaders, like Kapil Dev's, blends unshakable self-belief with the courage to defy odds. It's about rallying your team (or children) when hope seems lost, turning setbacks into comebacks through sheer persistence, and making bold, heart-driven decisions that logic might dismiss. Just as India's underdog triumph rewrote cricket history, great leaders don't wait for perfect conditions; they create them by stimulating conviction, strategic grit, and the mindset that every challenge is a pitch waiting to be hit out of the park.

3

A Letter from the Heart

"Not every star shines the brightest, but even the quietest light can guide the way." - Unknown

Dear Madam,

In a classroom of 30 to 40 students, I truly understand the challenge you face. So many young minds, so many needs, and so little time—it must be overwhelming. Among this crowd, I know it's difficult to notice every child. But I write to you today not with complaint, but with hope—hope that my voice, and more importantly, my child's spirit, won't go unnoticed forever.

You see, my son is what most would call "an average child," whom people usually fail to notice as he is neither at the top nor at the bottom. But the one who tries hard, smiles often, and quietly contributes in ways that go unseen?

People often ask me, *"Is your son good at math?"* or *"He's always in a sports uniform—he must be a great player, right?"*

And I smile and say, *"No, not really."* And honestly, I don't feel bad when I say that. I don't feel disappointed. I don't expect him to be the best at everything. And perhaps, neither should you.

I understand it's hard to notice a child who:

- Sits quietly and listens without always raising his hand.
- Who never asks questions (as his questions are beyond the syllabus, and when asked teacher often neglects him).
- Who is always part of the back-end team, helping huge background art sets for the sports day or preparing for the science demos.
- Plays the piano only in music class, but when his friends ask him to, he does so modestly.
- He always cheers from the sidelines, but a quiet, proud member of the cricket and football teams.
- Who cooks well and participates enthusiastically in culinary events.

It's okay if he is not noticeable in the crowd, it's okay that even if you fail to notice his sweet smile, funny talks, friendly personality, kind behaviour, mild manners, helpful nature, because he is just an average child. But what's *not* okay is the silent message he receives each day:

- That he is "just" an average student.

- That his life would be difficult if he did not score around 90% marks in exams.
- That his life would be miserable if he did not excel in sports.
- That life doesn't reward the mediocre child like him.

These are the thoughts that hurt him more than any bad grade ever could.

As his mother, I can accept his average scores. I can accept that he may not bring home medals or trophies. But what I cannot bear is the possibility of watching him lose his spark and self-esteem. I cannot watch him question his worth, courage, and confidence, simply because he does not shine in the usual ways.

Please, don't take away the quiet confidence he has built. Don't dim the light of his kindness, his innocence, his friendly spirit, his gentle strength. These are not average qualities. These are extraordinary human gifts.

So, dear teacher, I am not asking you to change the world for him. I am only asking you to *see* him. To notice the child who tries, who helps, who smiles, and who dares to be himself in a world pushing him to be someone else.

Because sometimes, the most average child carries the most extraordinary soul.

Thank you,

A proud mom of an "average" child.

Figure 3: A Letter to the Teacher

Key Points on Leadership:

Leadership is not about only rewarding the high achievers or the ones in the spotlight, but about valuing the quiet contributors, the steady helpers, and the kind hearts who lead through service, humility, and quiet strength. A great leader like a great teacher or parent, creates space for every individual to be seen, heard, and valued.

4

Parenting the Krishna Way

"Let us not raise children who seek perfection, but children who walk with purpose, act with love, and live with the wisdom of Krishna in their hearts." - Unknown

In a world where parenting is often shaped by pressure, competition, and fear of failure, the teachings of **Lord Krishna** offer a timeless path filled with grace, purpose, and peace. Krishna is not just a deity—he is a master communicator, a compassionate friend, a fearless warrior, a divine strategist, and above all, a **spiritual guide** for every parent.

As parents, we can learn to nurture our children in the light of his teachings, not just with rules and routines, but with soul-touching wisdom and values that anchor them for life. Let's learn the values of Krishna in the following steps.

1. PASSION IN CHAOS: NEVER LET GO OF WHAT YOU LOVE

Teach your children that no matter how turbulent life becomes, they must never abandon their hobbies and passions. Krishna played the flute even during times of war. His music was his soul's language—a stress-buster, a healer, a friend. Help your child find their own 'flute'—be it painting, music, writing, or dance—and never let them lose that joyful refuge. That spark keeps the soul alive.

2. KARMA WITH DETACHMENT: DOING WITHOUT CLINGING

Krishna taught Arjuna the meaning of *karma*—to act with integrity and sincerity but without attachment to the results. As parents, we must pass this on. Let your children know that what matters most is not success or applause, but honest effort and inner peace. Let them act, learn, fall, and rise—not for rewards, but for growth.

3. SERVE HUMANITY, SERVE GOD

One of Krishna's earliest lessons came when he saved the people of Vrindavan from poisoned waters. Service to the people is the purest form of worship. Encourage your child to be kind, helpful, and to serve others selflessly. These little acts of compassion lay the foundation for true greatness.

4. LIVE IN THE NOW: THE GIFT OF PRESENCE

Krishna lived each moment with full awareness. Teach your children to **live in the present**—not haunted by the past, nor anxious about the future. Life's challenges can seem intimidating, but if they face each day as it comes, with courage and presence, they will discover unimaginable strength within.

5. HUMILITY IN GREATNESS

Though divine, Krishna was humble. He treated everyone, regardless of age or status, with warmth and respect. He always showed respect for his parents, teachers, and elders. Let's raise children who don't measure their worth by achievements, but by the size of their hearts and wisdom.

6. SMILING THROUGH ADVERSITY

Krishna's smile never faded, even in adversity. Teach children to wear joy on their faces—not a forced grin, but a deep inner calm. Let them know that happiness is not the absence of trouble, but the presence of strength.

7. TRUE FRIENDSHIP KNOWS NO STATUS

The bond between Krishna and Sudama is a divine reminder that friendship is built on love, not labels. Raise your children to choose friends by heart, not caste, creed, or wealth. Respect and loyalty are what make friendships eternal.

8. DHARMA OVER DIFFICULTY: DOING THE RIGHT THING

Krishna's life was filled with moments where he stood up for what was right, like protecting Draupadi in her moment of humiliation. Teach your child that doing the right thing may be hard, lonely, and even thankless, but it is always worth it. Let them walk the path of **dharma**, guided by inner truth.

9. FACE CHALLENGES WITH STRATEGY, NOT PANIC

The battlefield of life requires more than courage, it needs **wisdom**. Krishna, the master strategist, teaches us to think beyond the obvious, to understand people deeply, and to respond with mindfulness. Help your children cultivate emotional intelligence and practical thinking, so they learn to adapt and overcome on difficult situations.

10. THE JOY OF GIVING

From the mischief of sharing butter with his friends to the divine act of sharing the *Bhagavad Gita* with the world, Krishna teaches us the joy of giving. Encourage your child to share, whether it's toys, food, time, or knowledge. In giving, we grow.

11. STAND BY YOUR PRINCIPLES AND GOALS

Krishna's life was anchored by clear goals:

- *Paritranaaya Sadhunam* – To protect the good
- *Vinashaaya Dushkritam* – To destroy evil
- *Dharma Samsthapanarthaya* – To reestablish righteousness

He stayed true to these principles at every stage of life. Likewise, let your child set **values-based goals**. Not every dream should be about achievement, some should be about **meaning**. Let them know: your goals shape who you become.

12. BE THE EXAMPLE YOU WISH TO TEACH

At just 12, Krishna fought injustice. He protected his parents, respected his elders, and supported his teachers. As parents, we must model the very values we wish to instill—respect, sacrifice, kindness, and courage. Our children are always watching, learning not just from our words, but from our choices.

Raising a child the *Krishna way* is not about religion; it's about **spiritual intelligence**, **emotional balance**, and **moral strength**. It is about nurturing human beings who know how to love, lead, laugh, and live with purpose.

May we raise not perfect children, but wise, kind, and courageous ones, who walk on the path of Krishna's ways.

Figure 4: Parenting the Krishna Way

Key Points on Leadership:

Krishna embodies the essence of true leadership—guiding with wisdom, courage, and compassion while staying rooted in dharma (righteousness). He taught Arjuna to act selflessly, prioritize duty over personal gain, and face challenges with strategic clarity. A leader, like Krishna, serves others selflessly (as seen in his protection of Vrindavan and Draupadi), remains humble despite greatness, and inspires through both words and actions. True leadership is not about authority but about empowering others, making principled decisions, and balancing strength with kindness, just as Krishna did on the battlefield of life.

5

Krishna – A Guide Amidst the Storm

*"Man needs his difficulties because they are necessary to enjoy success." - **Dr. A.P.J. Abdul Kalam***

The COVID-19 pandemic will forever remain etched in our collective memory as a time of uncertainty, fear, and solitude. It was more than a global health crisis; it was a deeply personal one, especially for our children. For over 60 days, our homes became classrooms, playgrounds, and sanctuaries. But behind the closed doors and glowing laptop screens, an invisible struggle was brewing in the minds of our young ones.

Children full of life, energy, and dreams found themselves confined within walls. Their laughter on playgrounds was replaced by silence, their curiosity boxed into online classes, and their emotional needs often met with impatience. Many of them became restless, low on confidence, and in many cases, on the verge of depression. While some signs were subtle, others were alarming. The toll on their mental and physical health was real and heavy.

Amidst this storm, another challenge quietly crept in: *the weight of parental expectations.* Parents, caught in the whirlwind of their own anxieties, began comparing their children with others. Education took center stage, but not in a nurturing way. The focus was on performance, results, and constant advice, often mistaken as quality time. In this chaos, the essence of connection was lost. Children, instead of being seen as individuals, became vessels for unrealized ambitions.

And yet, in times like these, the timeless wisdom of Krishna glows like a lamp in the dark.

Let us, as parents, take a moment to reflect—not just on Krishna, the God, but Krishna, the child raised by two sets of loving parents. King Vasudeva and Devaki trusted in the divine destiny of their son. Nandji and Yashoda poured love, joy, and trust into his upbringing. They gave him the freedom to grow, to play, to learn, and to *be*. Today, we must ask ourselves, do we offer our children the same?

Krishna's life is a lesson in perseverance, poise, and purpose. Even amidst war, betrayal, and adversity, he never let go of his inner calm. He played the flute not as an escape, but as a reminder of balance. His serenity wasn't just divine—it was deliberate. It was a choice to remain composed even when everything around him was falling apart.

This is what we must teach our children: that life will test them, but their spirit must not break.

Let us narrate to them the stories of Krishna's strength, not his miracles, but his mindset. Let them know that even God had to leave his home, fight battles, and face unfairness. Yet, he never gave up. He smiled through storms, danced through danger, and walked the path of dharma without fear.

Figure 5: Krishna- A Guide Amidst the Storm

We must remind them that happiness comes from within, not from marks, medals, or medals of approval. That adversities don't define them; how they respond to them does. That true strength is not in avoiding life's hardships but in facing them with grace.

Most importantly, let us remind ourselves, our children are not projects to perfect but souls to guide.

Every Janmashtami, let us invoke Krishna not just in temples, but in our homes, in our hearts, and most importantly—in our parenting. May his life continue to teach us to raise our children with compassion, patience, and unshakeable faith.

Let Krishna's flute echo through our homes again, bringing calm amidst chaos, joy amidst fear, and love amidst expectation.

Key Points on Leadership:

Amidst the pandemic's chaos, children needed anchors, not added pressure. Krishna's life reminds us that leadership in parenting (or any role) means building resilience through trust, not control. He faced adversity with a flute in hand and dharma in heart, teaching that real leadership lies in uplifting others, listening to their struggles, shielding their spirits, and lighting the way with compassion, not comparison. Like Krishna during the Mahabharata or in Vrindavan's storms, a leader's role isn't to eliminate challenges but to help others navigate them with courage, joy, and inner clarity.

6

The Race We Never Chose

"The best kind of parent you can be is to lead by example—love yourself, and your child will learn to do the same." - Brené Brown

As parents, especially mothers, we often find ourselves caught in a never-ending race, not just for survival, but for perfection. We chase the image of being a *better mom*, a *better spouse*, a *better daughter*, a *better homemaker*. We strive to become a "better version" of ourselves, but somewhere in this constant striving, the essence of *who we truly are* gets lost.

The world around us tells us to upgrade, improve, and outshine. Social media showcases curated moments of flawless parenting, perfect homes, and smiling children. It's hard not to compare. We begin to question ourselves: *"Am I doing enough?" "Am I falling short?"* And without even realizing it, we put on a mask, suppressing the raw, honest, beautifully flawed version of ourselves.

But pause and ask: why are we doing this? Who is this "better" version we are chasing? And who said that we are not already enough?

Parenting is not about perfection. It's about presence. It's about showing up every single day, with all our flaws, fatigue, love, and laughter. When we spend every moment trying to prove ourselves, we miss out on what truly matters: *being emotionally available for our children.* They don't need a "better" parent; they need *you,* your hugs, your stories, your values, your time.

Comparison is a thief not only of joy, but of self-worth. If we constantly compare our parenting journey to others, we unconsciously pass this mindset to our children. We teach them that love and value are earned, not inherent. They must *do* something to *be* someone. But isn't our real goal to raise children who love themselves, believe in their uniqueness, and thrive in their individuality?

To do that, we must begin by loving ourselves first. Accept the days when you feel drained. Celebrate the little wins. Forgive yourself for the yelling, the guilt, the unwashed dishes, and the skipped bedtime story. Parenting is messy, imperfect, and relentless, but it is also beautiful beyond measure.

So stop trying to be a better you. Start being you. The real you. The one your child looks up to, even on your worst days.

Because when you truly accept and love yourself, you raise children who do the same. And there is no greater legacy than that.

Figure 6: Stop Chasing Better. Start Being You

Key Points on Leadership:

True leadership begins with authenticity, not chasing perfection, but embracing your real, imperfect self with compassion. Just as children need parents who show up as they are, great leaders inspire by being genuine, vulnerable, and emotionally present. When we let go of comparison and self-doubt, we model self-worth and teach others to lead from their core values, not external validation. Leadership, like parenting, isn't about flawless performance; it's about guiding with love and the courage to be unapologetically *you.*

7

The Leap Year Gift – One Extra Day to Love

*"Wherever you are, and whatever you do, be in love." - **Rumi***

Every four years, the universe gifts us something precious—an extra day. Just one more day. But within it lies 24 hours, 1,440 minutes, and 86,400 seconds, a treasure trove of time we so often wish we had more of. In our fast-paced lives filled with deadlines, responsibilities, and to-do lists, this extra day feels like a gentle nudge from the cosmos, reminding us of what truly matters: time with our children.

What if, instead of letting this bonus day slip by like any other, we *celebrated* it? Embraced it as a sacred pause—a chance to reconnect, rediscover, and rejoice in the little moments with our kids?

Let's call it what it is: a gift. And if the 29th of February lands on a weekend, that gift is wrapped in laughter, sprinkled with joy, and tied with the ribbon of togetherness.

WHY THIS DAY MATTERS

Our calendar was never perfect. Earth takes approximately 365.25 days to orbit the Sun. To balance the books, Julius Caesar decreed in 45 B.C. that an extra day be added every four years. What he didn't know was that, centuries later, this bonus day would mean something far more emotional than just correcting a calendar—it would become a day where we could pause.

So, how do we make the most of it as parents? How do we turn these extra 86,400 seconds into golden memories?

IDEAS TO TURN TIME INTO LOVE

1. **Be a Child Again – Let's Play!**
   Cast aside adulthood for a day. Build a fort, play tag, jump on the trampoline, or get messy with clay. Laugh loud, run wild. Let your child see not just your face, but your *heart*—the one that still remembers how to play.
2. **Paint the Day**
   Pick up crayons, watercolors, or colored pencils—whatever's around. Create silly art, paint handprints, or doodle the day away. This isn't about skill. It's about **connection**. You'll be surprised how much a child reveals through colors and brush strokes—their dreams, fears, and joys.
3. **Visit a Fun Zone – And Actually Play**
   Not just supervise. Participate. Whether it's arcade games, go-kart racing, or a round of air hockey, be their teammate. The thrill on their faces, the shared

cheers, the bursts of laughter—these are moments that etch themselves in your child's heart forever.

4. **Gift a Book, Share a World**
   Choose a storybook, a comic, or an adventure novel. Curl up together, voices low. Let your child's imagination bloom, and yours too. Storytime becomes soul time.
5. **Make Your Own List**
   Perhaps you want to bake cookies together. Or dance to your childhood favorites. Or plant something in the garden. Whatever it is, do it with intention, do it with love.

Figure 7: The Leap Year Gift

THE REAL GIFT OF FEBRUARY 29

This bonus day isn't just about what we do—it's about what we *feel*. It's about showing our kids that while the world moves fast, we can still pause. That they are *worth* our undivided time. That one day can create a lifetime memory.

As parents, we don't often get to slow down. But maybe every four years, the universe conspires to give us a little time back. And when it does, let's not waste it. Let's hold our children a little tighter, laugh a little louder, and love a little deeper.

Because someday, when our kids are grown, they might just look back and say,

"Do you remember that Leap Year Day we spent together? That was the best day ever."

Key Points on Leadership:

As a leader, you need to turn fleeting moments into lasting impact by prioritizing connection over productivity. Just as the extra day of a leap year offers a rare chance to pause and invest wholly in our children, great leaders understand that their most meaningful influence comes not from grand gestures but from undivided attention and shared joy. When we lead with time and heart, we don't just manage moments; we create legacies of love and belonging.

8

A Mother's Nurturing Touch

"Strong roots produce beautiful branches. Give your child the gift of struggle, and they will find their own strength."- Unknown

The other day, I found myself observing the quiet corners of my home — not the walls or the décor, but a small family of money plants I've been growing for the past few months in simple glass bottles. They've become part of my everyday rhythm, watering them, turning their leaves toward the sun, wiping the glass jars clean. Yet, something caught my attention. A curious contrast.

Some of these plants were flourishing, stretching out fresh green leaves as if dancing to their own silent song. Others stood still, no new leaves, no fresh growth. And I began to wonder: I give them the same care, same water, same light, same manure. Then why are only a few of them growing, while the others remain unchanged?

That's when I noticed the roots of the thriving ones that I had gently peeled or slightly torn at the base before placing in water, a small effort, a deliberate gesture. They had gone through a little pain. But they had responded to it. They had grown stronger.

And then, as a mother, it struck me.

Isn't this true for our children too?

We nurture them with love, attention, and resources, but it's the small challenges we give them, the little stings of discipline, the nudges to take responsibility that become the roots of their future resilience.

Just like those plants, our children need time, care, and sometimes, that extra push to step out of their comfort zone. They may resist. They may cry or become restless. And yet, when we ask them to try again, to face a challenge, to work hard, we're not being harsh. We're helping them grow roots.

Because success isn't always the point. Growth is.

When a child learns to take on a small challenge, they learn to believe in their ability. If they succeed, they build confidence. If they fail, they discover the world doesn't end; that failure is not defeat but a stepping stone. And they try again. What we're really doing is helping them lay a foundation that can withstand the storms of life.

The ones with strong roots shoot up faster. Not because they are different, but because they are prepared.

So, the next time we feel the ache of watching our child struggle, whether with schoolwork, a friendship, or a new responsibility, let's remember that it's part of their rooting.

Our care, our silent sacrifices, our steady encouragement, these are the nutrients.

The growth may not be visible every day. But one morning, you'll see new leaves.

And just like those plants by the window, your child will reach for the sun, confident, grounded, and full of life.

Figure 8: The Mother's Nurturing Touch

Key Points on Leadership:

Leadership, like nurturing a plant, requires the wisdom to balance care with challenge, knowing when to provide support and when to gently push others beyond their comfort zones. Just as plants grow stronger when their roots face resistance, children (and teams) flourish when given space to struggle, fail, and persevere. A leader's role isn't to eliminate obstacles but to encourage development, trusting that short-term discomfort cultivates long-term strength. The greatest growth often emerges not from constant protection, but from the courage to let others stretch their roots.

9

The Power of One More Push

"Our greatest glory is not in never falling, but in rising every time we fall."- Confucius

We often teach our children not to give up, to keep going even when things get tough. But how many times do we, as parents, truly live by that lesson ourselves?

A famous poem by John Greenleaf Whittier echoes in my mind:

"When things go wrong as they sometimes will,
When the road you're trudging seems all uphill...
Rest if you must, but don't you quit..
Don't give up, though the pace seems slow..."

We've read these words countless times on bookmarks, on a classroom wall, in WhatsApp forwards. But how often do we truly live them? More importantly, how often do we pass this strength on to our children?

Let me take you to a moment that brought this lesson back to life for me, not as a quote, but as a reality.

During one of my yoga sessions, my instructor asked me to perform 20 rounds of Suryanamaskar. I nodded, full of confidence. But by the 7th round, my breath grew heavy, my legs felt weak, and a loud voice echoed inside me, "Stop. You can't go on. Just sit down. You've done enough."

That voice was tempting. Comforting. It was telling me what I *wanted* to hear. But then came another voice, softer but firm, "Don't quit. Push a little more. You can do it."

And I did. I pushed forward, and by the end of it, I had completed 25 rounds, something I didn't believe I was capable of.

And in that moment, I realized: this was not just about yoga. It was parenting in its purest metaphor.

How many times do our children want to quit? When the math homework overwhelms them, when the game isn't going in their favor, when they want to give up on learning to ride a bicycle, or when failure shakes their spirit?

It's not about forcing them relentlessly. It's about gently guiding them to believe in their own resilience. To teach them that failure is not final. That resting is okay, but quitting, especially without trying one more time, is the only real defeat.

When children begin to recognize that growth lies just beyond their comfort zone, they stop fearing struggle. They learn to embrace effort, to build grit, and eventually, they start carrying their own inner voice of strength. That's when they begin to discover their full potential.

So the next time your child says, “I can’t do it,” be that second voice. Whisper this:

“Yes, you can. Don’t quit now. Just push a little more.”

Because it’s in that extra try, that one more push, that true growth and magic happen.

Figure 9: The Power of One More Push

Key Points on Leadership:

A leader recognizes the pivotal moment when someone is on the verge of giving up and inspires them to push just one step further. Like a parent encouraging a struggling child or a yoga instructor guiding a student past their perceived limits, great leaders don't accept "I can't" as final; they help others discover that breakthrough often waits just beyond comfort's edge. This isn't about relentless pressure, but about instilling resilient mindsets - teaching that rest is allowed but surrender isn't an option, because true potential reveals itself when we dare to try "one more time."

10

That Little Extra Push is a Key to Your Success

"Children must be taught how to think, not what to think."- Margaret Mead

One morning at the gym, I ran into a friend who looked particularly stressed. His teenage son wanted to attend a cricket match happening the next day, and he hadn't managed to book the tickets online. Guilt had taken over him.

He was cursing himself for being careless with the desire of the kid. Due to all this, he was feeling as if he had committed some crime by not being able to arrange for the ticket to the cricket match for the kid.

This small interaction got me thinking.

As parents, we are constantly bombarded with our children's wants, not always needs, just wants. Chocolates, ice creams, that new toy a friend flaunted at school, a T-shirt worn by their favorite YouTuber, a trip to a fancy café, or the latest game trending online. And most of us try hard to give them what they ask for. We stretch ourselves emotionally, mentally, sometimes even financially, to fulfill these requests. We do it out of love. Out of care. Out of a desire to be the best parent we can be.

But here's where the problem begins: we equate being a "good parent" with being a "super parent."

We forget that we are human, not superheroes. And we fall into a dangerous trap: the trap of guilt and comparison. A trap where we start feeling like failures if we can't meet every demand or desire of our child. But we must break free from it. Because parenting isn't about being perfect, it's about being real, grounded, and emotionally available.

We need to teach our children something far more valuable than indulgence: we need to teach them to understand the difference between need and desire, between wish and necessity. They must know that it's okay not to get everything they ask for.

Saying "no" occasionally is not a sign of failure. It is, in fact, an act of love. It teaches our children resilience. It teaches them patience. It builds their ability to cope with disappointments, something life will hand them in plenty.

Let your children see the real you, not the version that constantly tries to keep up with every whim or expectation. Let them see a parent who is honest, loving, emotionally strong, and deeply human. Teach them the value of contentment and the joy of gratitude. Help them love you for your presence, your values, your principles, not just for the things you buy them or the wishes you fulfill.

In this super-materialistic world, your greatest gift to your child is helping them realize that love is not transactional. You don't have to wear a cape to be loved. You just have to show up with truth, time, and tenderness.

Because your role is not to be a superhuman…

Your role is to be their parent. Just that, and it is more than enough.

Figure 10: You Don't have to be a Superparent

Key Points on Leadership:

True leadership, like parenting, isn't about fulfilling every demand or appearing infallible; it's about having the courage to say "no" when needed, setting boundaries with love, and teaching others to distinguish between wants and needs. Just as children grow through learning patience when desires go unfulfilled, teams thrive under leaders who prioritize values over validation, emotional presence over perfection, and long-term growth over short-term gratification. The strongest leaders, like the wisest parents, understand that real influence comes not from being a superhero, but from showing up authentically, with both compassion and clarity.

11

Give Wings to Fly and Let Her Soar

"We cannot all succeed when half of us are held back."- Malala Yousafzai

Before starting this chapter, let's read the following lines of *Rumi* that align with the theme of this chapter.

God has created
your wings not to be dormant
as long as you are alive
you must try more and more
to use your wings to show you're alive
these wings of yours
are filled with quests and hopes
if they are not used
they will wither away
*they will soon decay..-**Rumi***

There was a time when young girls, especially in our generation, grew up without ever being asked a simple, powerful question: *What do you want to become?* We were taught to be obedient, to follow the path laid out by others, to shrink our dreams if they did not align with tradition.

But I was fortunate. I was one of the few whose parents asked me what *I* liked, what subjects stirred my curiosity, and what profession I dreamed of. They allowed me to choose my stream and stand by my ambitions. And you know what that gave me? Not just a career—it gave me a voice, a confidence, a backbone. It gave me the power to stand tall when life tried to bend me.

Yet, the world beyond home wasn't as kind. As a woman, society looked at my dreams with suspicion. I was labeled "too ambitious," as though wanting to work, contribute, and grow was something to be ashamed of. After marriage, though my family supported me, society frowned upon my choices. But I didn't let it pull me down. I worked. I raised a family. I balanced both. I didn't chase ambition at the cost of my loved ones, but I didn't give up on myself either.

Now, years later, I look at my daughter, my beautiful, fierce teenager, with a fire in her eyes that reminds me of my younger self. But this time, I don't want history to repeat. I want her wings to be even stronger than mine. I want her dreams to be limitless, not tucked away in the corners of compromise.

Figure 11: Give Wings to Fly and Let Her Soar

To my daughter and to every parent reading this—give your children the *sky*. Especially your daughters. Don't clip their wings with doubt, fear, or outdated expectations. Give them roots in values, yes, but wings to fly—boldly, beautifully, beyond what even you imagined.

Let them know that their dreams are valid. That ambition is not arrogance. That they can be both compassionate and courageous, nurturing and unstoppable. Teach them that their identity is not tied to roles they play for others, but in the dreams they dare to live for themselves.

Let us not just raise daughters who are 'good.' Let us raise daughters who are free.

Key Points on Leadership:

Parenting means empowering your tiny tots and helping them to discover and pursue their own aspirations, not just follow predetermined paths. Just as the author's parents nurtured her dreams despite societal resistance, great leaders create environments where potential can soar by replacing limiting beliefs with trust, encouragement, and the courage to challenge conventions. Whether raising daughters or guiding teams, the most transformative leadership gives both roots (values) and wings (autonomy), understanding that real growth happens when we stop dictating trajectories and start clearing runways for others' unique ambitions to take flight.

12

Push Beyond the Limits – A Ride into the Unknown

"Sometimes, the best way to learn is to go beyond limits and set your own rules."- Unknown

Have you ever done something so bold, so out of your comfort zone, that even you questioned your sanity afterward?

Until recently, my answer to that question would've been a confident **"No."**

But life has a way of surprising you, especially when you dare to challenge it.

Just a few weeks ago, I did something most would call crazy: I rode 300 kilometers on a bicycle in one single night.

No medals. No media. No cheering crowd.

Just a personal war between me, the road, and the limits I thought I had.

HOW IT ALL STARTED

On 5th March, my coach casually told me,

"Ride at least 30 km daily for 30 days, with three major rides—100, 150, and 200 km—then talk to me."

That sentence didn't just challenge me, it hit my ego like a bullet.

The next day, on 6th March, without much thought or planning, I declared in my group:

"I'm doing 300 km. One go. Solo."

At that time, my longest ride had only been 160 km. Physically, I wasn't prepared. Mentally, I was unsure. Emotionally, I was fired up but even that has limits, as I'd soon learn.

THE ROAD AHEAD

This wasn't a cycling event with volunteers, pit stops, or traffic control. It was me, my cycle, the **night highway**.

The challenges?

1. **Riding solo at night** on highways lined with trucks and buses.
2. **No support system** if my tire punctured or something went wrong.
3. **The brutal heat** that made riding during the day impossible.

My mind screamed, *"Don't do it."* My heart whispered, *"You have to."*

So I made peace with two outcomes:

Either I'll end up in the hospital, or I'll complete it.

The parenting lessons I learned during this ride challenge are:

1. Fear is a Mind Game – Kids often fear failure, rejection, or embarrassment. Just like I had to ignore my fear of riding alone at night, children must learn that fear only grows if they feed it. Teach them: *"Feel the fear, but do it anyway."*

2. Commitment Builds Character – When children commit to something (a sport, a project, a habit), they learn accountability. If they want to quit, remind them: *"You promised yourself you'd try. Let's see it through."*

3. "Why" Isn't Always Enough – Kids (and adults) often give up when motivation fades. That's when we must help them find deeper reasons—*" love for the activity, or pride in effort"*.

4. Emotions Drive Persistence – Just as my anger and determination pushed me through exhaustion, children need emotional fuel. Encourage them with: *"You're stronger than you think. Keep going!"*

5. Even Emotions Have Limits – During my 300 km ride, after covering 100 km, I reached a point where all my 'whys,' emotions, and motivations failed me. I searched within for strength, but I realized that these things have their limits and could no longer push me forward. But the drive for one more step fueled me. Teach kids: *"When you don't feel like trying, just take one more step,"* and that's enough to keep them moving.

6. Persistence is the Ultimate Lesson – *"Keep doing what you're doing"*- this is the only mantra I learned that helped me complete the 300 km ride. The more you believe in this mantra, the more energy and satisfaction you gain. The mantra applies to parenting too. Whether it's homework, chores, or personal goals, consistency builds resilience.

Final Lesson: Let Them Struggle (With Love)

Just as I had to face exhaustion, uncertainty, and pain to finish my ride, children must experience struggle to grow. Don't rescue them too soon. Instead, be their coach, challenging, supporting, and believing in them even when they don't believe in themselves.

Figure 12: A Ride into the Unknown

Key Points on Leadership:

Enduring a 300km solo ride means guiding others to confront their self-imposed limits by showing them that breakthroughs happen when motivation fades but persistence remains. Just as the author discovered that emotions and "whys" have expiration dates, great leaders teach teams to rely on disciplined action ("just one more step") when inspiration runs dry. The real test of leadership isn't preventing struggle but walking alongside others in the trenches—challenging them to keep pedaling when every muscle screams stop, proving that limits are often just illusions waiting to be shattered by grit.

13

Unlearn Parenting – The Mission Mangal Way

"Parenting isn't about perfect answers—it's about being present in imperfect moments, with love loud enough to be heard beyond words." - Unknown

Parenting is often considered rocket science—complex and challenging. It's 1) difficult because there are no fixed rules; every situation and circumstance demands a different approach. It's 2) technical because you constantly have to learn, unlearn, and relearn. While watching the movie *Mission Mangal,* both of these notions about parenting were reaffirmed. The entire movie felt like a powerful lesson in parenting. Some of the most valuable parenting insights can be drawn from the following instances:

Ironically, while watching the film *Mission Mangal,* a movie about India's space triumph, I found myself absorbing some of the most profound lessons in parenting. Not from any book or parenting coach, but from a film about science, determination, and human emotion.

Here's how *Mission Mangal* turned into a powerful metaphor for what it truly means to raise a child in today's world.

1. HOME IS THE FIRST LAB, AND YOU ARE THE FIRST SCIENTIST

We're often told, *"Home is the first school,"* but it's more than that; home is also the first lab. And parents? We are the scientists.

In the movie, when the scientists faced a lack of resources, they turned to everyday solutions, like frying pooris to simulate thermal insulation. That creativity came not from the lab, but from the kitchen, from the **ordinary chaos of daily life**.

Likewise, parenting isn't about grand strategies. It's in the small, daily choices:

– How we respond when our child breaks something.

– How we explain failure.

– How we model patience.

Every action teaches. Every word echoes.

You are your child's most important teacher, even when you don't realise you're teaching.

2. GIVE THEM SPACE TO BREATHE, TO BECOME

There's a moment in *Mission Mangal* when Tara's teenage son expresses a desire to become a musician and starts studying the Quran because he admires A.R. Rahman. In that moment, Tara doesn't scream, argue, or impose. She listens.

She asks. She learns why.

As parents, our first reaction is often fear: *"What's happening to my child?"* But Tara shows us something profound: Curiosity is more powerful than control.

Instead of reacting, she responded with calm. Instead of forcing, she guided.

Our job is not to shape them into who we want. It's to give them the space to discover who they are.

3. DON'T DISMISS. ENGAGE. LET CURIOSITY LEAD

When her son wanted to follow a different faith, Tara didn't ridicule the idea. She engaged. She allowed him to explore, and then gently helped him understand the deeper aspects of religion.

Today's kids are not afraid to ask "why." They need answers that make sense, not just rules.

Parenting today isn't about commanding obedience. It's about building trust. And that trust comes when you choose conversation over confrontation.

4. OBSERVE WITHOUT INVADING – WATCH WITHOUT JUDGMENT

There's a fine line between watching over and spying on your children. The difference lies in intention.

Keep an eye but not with suspicion. With love. With quiet presence.

Be the kind of parent who notices but doesn't intrude. Let your children feel safe, not watched.

Be their safety net, not their surveillance camera.

5. SPEAK ABOUT YOUR LIFE – MAKE THEM PART OF YOUR WORLD

One beautiful message in the movie is the bond Tara shares with her children. She doesn't shield them from her work instead, she shares stories. She explains her mission.

And through this, a bridge is built. When you talk to your children about your passions, challenges, and goals, they begin to respect your time, your work, and your identity beyond parenting.

Inclusion breeds understanding. Understanding breeds connection.

6. CHILDREN LEARN WHAT YOU LIVE

Kids are always watching.

They pick up on your words, your tone, the way you treat the waiter, and how you react when things don't go your way. Your values are not taught, they are absorbed.

Every day, they are unconsciously asking:

"How do we deal with stress?"

"How do we love?"

"What do we do when things go wrong?"

Your answer? It's not what you say. It's what you do.

7. BE THE ROLE MODEL – NOT THE PERFECTIONIST

You don't need to be the perfect parent. You need to be a present parent.

Let them see you fail, get up, and try again. Let them witness your effort, your grind, your sincerity.

Success is secondary. What matters most is showing them the dignity in trying. The grace in effort.

8. LEAVE THE BAGGAGE AT THE DOOR – COME HOME, FULLY

Tara, despite her professional pressures, never brought the weight of her job back home. This is a beautiful reminder: Our children don't need us to be superhuman. They need us to be fully human.

Present. Attentive. Warm.

Let the home be a sanctuary. Not an extension of your office or your stress.

When you enter your home, change roles. Be a mom. Be a hug. Be a haven.

9. CELEBRATE WITH THEM – BECOME PART OF THEIR JOY

When Tara visits her daughter at a pub, she doesn't scold or shame her. She observes quietly and then chooses to join the celebration, not ruin it. She even brings her husband into the moment, building a bond that had been missing.

That's the magic of parenting—when you step into their world, even for a moment, you create memories they'll treasure.

Be the bridge—not the wall—between them and the world.

FINAL REFLECTION: PARENTING IS A MISSION

Just like *Mission Mangal,* parenting requires:

- Vision
- Patience
- Teamwork
- Resilience
- Innovation

It's a journey of unlearning what we thought we knew, and embracing a new way of raising children, one that's rooted in *connection, curiosity, and compassion.*

So, unlearn the rules. Relearn your child.

And remember: *You're not raising a robot. You're raising a soul.*

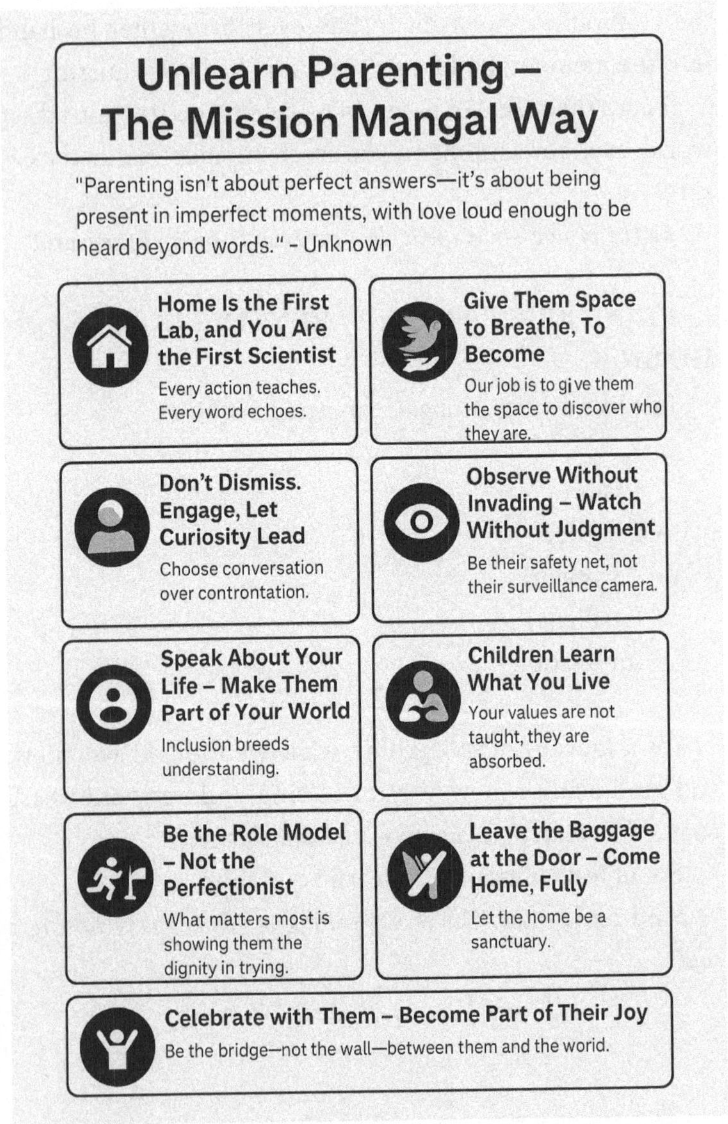

Figure 13: Unlearn Parenting – The Mission Mangal Way

Key Points on Leadership:

A great leader turns everyday moments into "launch pads" for growth. Just as Tara balanced rocket science with raising teens, leaders thrive when they: listen like a student (not just instruct), problem-solve with kitchen-table creativity, and protect their team's dreams as fiercely as their own mission. Because whether guiding a space program or a child, real impact happens when you replace "Because I said so" with "Let's figure this out together."

14

Conclusion

"There can be no keener revelation of a society's soul than the way in which it treats its children" - Nelson Mandela

As this book draws to a close, it's important to remember that parenting doesn't.

Parenting is not a chapter we finish. It is a lifelong script we co-write with our children, filled with love, mistakes, discovery, growth, and above all, connection.

Throughout these chapters, we've explored how to raise not just successful children, but whole-hearted human beings.

LEGACY IS NOT WHAT YOU LEAVE BEHIND-IT'S WHAT YOU RAISE

What you give your child is more than food, shelter, or education.

You give them their first definition of love.

You give them the foundation of their self-worth.

You give them the courage to rise after failure, and the grace to stay humble after success.

Your legacy is not in what you build. It's in who you raise.

So raise with intention. Discipline with love. Correct with compassion. And connect with truth.

Let your home be the first place your child learns values not because you taught them, but because you lived them.

THE LEADER YOU RAISE TOMORROW BEGINS WITH THE LOVE YOU GIVE TODAY

The world your child is stepping into is fast, competitive, and complex. But within your home, let them find simplicity, strength, and safety. Let them find faith in themselves, inspired by your belief in them.

Let them grow roots deep in values. And let them grow wings, fueled by your trust.

Because one day, when they step into the world not just to survive, but to lead, it won't be their grades or gadgets that define them.

It will be the character you nurtured, the resilience you modeled, and the love you gave unconditionally.

So here's to raising not perfect children, but powerful souls.

Here's to Raising Tomorrow's Leader with heart, with hope, and with honour.

Please send me your feedback on this book to my email at garjana.rathore@gmail.com. I look forward to hearing from you.

Figure 14: From Roots to Wings- Parenting Legacy

15

Book References

1. Bhagavad Gita (Translated by Eknath Easwaran). Easwaran, E. (2007). The Bhagavad Gita (2nd ed.). Nilgiri Press.

2. Brown, B.(2012). Daring greatly: How the courage to be vulnerable transforms the way we live, love, parent, and lead. Gotham Books.

3. Cain, S.(2012). Quiet: The power of introverts in a world that can't stop talking. Crown Publishers.

4. David, S. (2016). Emotional agility: Get unstuck, embrace change, and thrive in work and life. Avery.

5. Duckworth, A. (2016). Grit: The power of passion and perseverance. Scribner.

6. Dweck, C. S. (2006). Mindset: The new psychology of success. Random House.

7. Jeffers, S. (1987). Feel the fear and do it anyway. Ballantine Books.

8. Kerr, J. (2013). Legacy: What the All Blacks can teach us about the business of life. Constable.

9. Lahey, J. (2015). The gift of failure: How the best parents learn to let go so their children can succeed. HarperCollins.

10. Lythcott-Haims, J. (2015). How to raise an adult: Break free of the overparenting trap and prepare your kid for success. Henry Holt and Co.

11. Obama, M. (2018). Becoming. Crown Publishing.

12. Perry, P. (2019). The book you wish your parents had read (and your children will be glad that you did). Penguin Life.

13. Siegel, D. J., & Payne Bryson, T. (2011). The whole-brain child: 12 revolutionary strategies to nurture your child's developing mind. Delacorte Press.

14. Tolle, E. (2004). The power of now: A guide to spiritual enlightenment. New World Library.

15. Tough, P. (2012). How children succeed: Grit, curiosity, and the hidden power of character. Houghton Mifflin Harcourt..

16

Recommended Reading List

1. Parenting with Purpose & Resilience

- The Gift of Failure by Jessica Lahey
- Mindset: The New Psychology of Success by Carol S. Dweck
- The Whole-Brain Child by Daniel J. Siegel and Tina Payne Bryson
- How to Raise an Adult by Julie Lythcott-Haims

2. Leadership & Life Lessons from Sports

- Relentless: From Good to Great to Unstoppable by Tim S. Grover
- Legacy: What the All Blacks Can Teach Us About the Business of Life by James Kerr
- Open by Andre Agassi (Memoir on resilience and self-belief)

3. Emotional Intelligence & Inner Strength

- Emotional Agility by Susan David

- Raising Emotionally Strong Boys by David Thomas
- The Book You Wish Your Parents Had Read by Philippa Perry

4. Ancient Wisdom for Modern Parenting

- The Bhagavad Gita (Eknath Easwaran's translation)
- Krishna: The Man and His Philosophy by Osho
- The Art of Happiness by Dalai Lama & Howard Cutler

5. Nurturing Individuality & Self-Worth

- Quiet: The Power of Introverts in a World That Can't Stop Talking by Susan Cain
- Daring Greatly by Brené Brown
- The Self-Driven Child by William Stixrud and Ned Johnson

6. Overcoming Fear & Building Grit

- Grit: The Power of Passion and Perseverance by Angela Duckworth
- Feel the Fear and Do It Anyway by Susan Jeffers
- Drive: The surprising truth about what motivates us

7. Mindfulness & Presence in Parenting

- The Power of Now by Eckhart Tolle
- Simplicity Parenting by Kim John Payne
- Present Over Perfect by Shauna Niequist

8. Raising Empowered Girls

- Becoming by Michelle Obama
- Dear Ijeawele, or A Feminist Manifesto in Fifteen Suggestions by Chimamanda Ngozi Adichie
- Girl, Stop Apologizing by Rachel Hollis

9. Books for Children (To Read Together)

- The Boy, the Mole, the Fox and the Horse by Charlie Mackesy
- What Do You Do With a Problem? by Kobi Yamada
- The Dot by Peter H. Reynolds (Creativity & self-belief)

17

Find Me Here

LinkedIn

https://www.linkedin.com/in/garjana-rathore-86914319/

Facebook

https://www.facebook.com/search/top?q=garjana%20rathore

9 789334 333879

Printed at Repro India Ltd.